CLARENCE THOMAS

THE

BIOGRAPHY

copyright© MARK LEWIS

2022

Table of Contents

INTRO

A member of the United States Supreme Court, Clarence Thomas was born on June 23, 1948, in Washington, D.C., and currently resides in Washington, D.C. As Thurgood Marshall's successor, he was appointed by President George H.W. Bush and has served since 1991. Second in line to serve after Marshall, Thomas is an African American. The Supreme Court's highest associate justice, Thomas, has been a member of the Court for almost 30 years as of 2018.

While attending Yale Law School, Thomas was exposed to the Gullah culture through his time at Holy Cross, where he was exposed to the Gullah language and culture. Following his 1974 appointment as an assistant attorney general in Missouri, he went into private practice. At the beginning of the 1980s, he was a legislative assistant to U.S. Senator John Danforth, and he was promoted to Assistant Secretary for Civil Rights at the U.S. Department of Education later that year. As a result of President Reagan's appointment, Thomas became the first African-American to head the Equal Employment Opportunity Commission (EEOC).

For the District of Columbia Circuit Court of Appeals, President George H. W. Bush nominated Thomas. When he was appointed to the Supreme Court, he served in that position for 16 months before taking on Marshall. The EEOC and the Department of Education both accused Thomas of harassing and sexually assaulting attorney Anita Hill during his confirmation hearings. In spite of Hill's repeated requests for him to cease,

Thomas allegedly made many sexual and romantic advances toward her. It was claimed by Thomas and his allies that Hill, as well as those who testified in support of her, manufactured the claims in order to block the confirmation of a black conservative to the Supreme Court. Thomas was confirmed by a 52–48 majority in the Senate.

Thomas's jurisprudence is described by Supreme Court scholars as an originalist, which emphasizes the original meaning of the United States Constitution and statutes. Before becoming a judge, he was also a supporter of natural law. According to many observers, Thomas is the most conservative member of the Supreme Court.

CHILDHOOD

The year was 1948 when Thomas was born in the predominantly black town of Pin Point, Georgia, which had been established by freedmen after the American Civil War. A farm worker and domestic worker, he was the second child of M. C. Thomas and Leola "Pigeon" Williams. The family was descended from slaves, and Gullah was the primary language of communication. Sandy and Peggy, two slaves, owned by wealthy planter Josiah Wilson of Liberty County, Georgia, were Thomas's first known ancestors. Early on, Thomas's ears began to ring. Father abruptly abandoned the family. Many times, despite Thomas's mother's best efforts, she was forced to rely on the generosity of strangers in order to put food on the table. The Andersons, Myers, and Christine (née Hargrove) Anderson welcomed Thomas and Myers into their home after a house fire left them homeless.

Afterward, Thomas was introduced to the conveniences of modern life, including indoor plumbing and regular meals.

Despite his lack of formal education, Myers Anderson built a successful fuel oil company that sold ice as well. Anderson has been referred to by Thomas as "the greatest man I have ever known." Every day from dawn to dusk, Anderson took Thomas and his family to work on a farm. Throughout his life, Anderson instilled in his children a strong sense of self-reliance and a belief in the power of hard work. He also stressed the importance of a good education to his grandchildren.

EDUCATION

Raised Catholic, Thomas went to St. Pius X High School for two years, where he was one of only a handful of black students, before transferring to St. John Vianney's Minor Seminary on the Isle of Hope.

A Roman Catholic seminary in Missouri, he also briefly attended Conception Seminary College for a brief period of time. Thomas was the only member of his family who had never gone to college. After the assassination of Martin Luther King, Jr., Thomas says he left the seminary. After the shooting, he heard another student say, "Good, I hope the son of a bitch died," and he didn't think the church was doing enough to fight racism.

Thomas became a sophomore transfer student at Worcester's College of the Holy Cross after a recommendation from a nun.

Thomas was an active member of the Black Student Union while attending the university. He once participated in a walkout of the school after some black students were disciplined while white students were not. Black students were allowed back into the school by some priests who worked out a deal with the protesters.

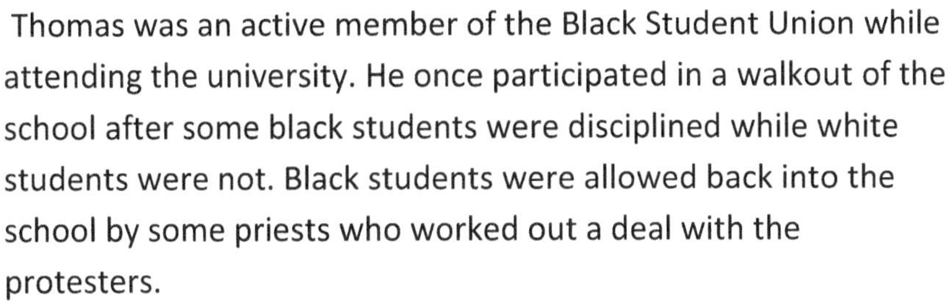

Thomas attended anti-war marches and witnessed the 1970 Harvard Square riots as a student, and he has said that these events sparked his disillusionment with leftist movements and his shift to the right.

Even though he had been drilled in grammar in school, Thomas, who grew up speaking Gullah, realized in college that his accent was still unpolished and decided to major in English literature "to conquer the language."

He was also a member of the Alpha Sigma Nu fraternity and the Purple Key Society while attending Holy Cross. Holy Cross alumnus Thomas graduated with a bachelor of arts degree in English literature in 1971.

As a student at Holy Cross, Thomas received several deferments from the military draft. On graduation, he received a low lottery number, which indicated he was at risk of being called up to serve in the Vietnam War. Thomas was not drafted because he failed his medical exam and had a curvature of the spine.

EDUCATION IN THE FIELD OF LAW

In 1974, Thomas graduated from Yale Law School with a Juris Doctor (J.D.) degree, placing him in the middle of his graduating class.

On the basis of affirmative action, Thomas believes that the law firms to which he applied for employment after graduating from Yale did not take his Juris Doctor degree seriously. In 1969, Yale Law's quota program for black applicants was expanding, with up to 24 students entering that year under a system that deemphasized grades and LSAT scores, according to Dean Louis Pollak. Furthermore, according to Thomas, "the law firms also asked pointed questions, unsubtly suggesting that they doubted my grades." Thomas wrote the following in his autobiography published in 2007: "To serve as a constant reminder of the blunder I'd made by attending Yale Law School, I affixed a fifteen-cent sticker to the frame of my law degree. I never doubted its importance."

INFLUENCES FROM THE WRITTEN WORD

After reading Thomas Sowell's Race and Economics in 1975, Thomas found an intellectual foundation for his philosophy.

Government social reform, this book argues for personal action to overcome adversity. It wasn't just The Fountainhead that influenced him; he made his staff watch the 1949 film adaptation of the novel. His "strong libertarian leanings" have been acknowledged by Thomas.

Richard Wright's books Native Son and Black Boy "capture[d] a lot of the feelings that I had inside that you learn how to repress," according to Thomas, who has said Wright is the most influential writer in his life.

Both Ralph Ellison's Invisible Man and Thomas's own Native Son are two of his all-time favorite books.

Thomas enjoys Spike Lee's films, particularly Malcolm X and Do the Right Thing. According to him, he would be delighted to have the opportunity to meet Lee.

CAREER

EARLY IN LIFE

In 1986, while serving as Chairman of the Equal Employment Opportunity Commission, Thomas met with President Ronald Reagan.

Thomas attended Saint Louis University School of Law after graduating, where he studied to become a lawyer in Missouri. On September 13, 1974, he was sworn in as a lawyer in Missouri. The state of Missouri appointed him an assistant attorney general from 1974 to 1977, working under fellow Yale alumnus John Danforth. Danforth's staff had only one other person of color, Thomas. Before moving on to the revenue and taxation division, he began his career in Danforth's office, first in the criminal appeals division. He has said that being Assistant Attorney General is the best job he has ever had in his entire career. In 1976, Danforth was elected to the Senate, and Thomas moved to St. Louis, Missouri, to work as an attorney for Monsanto Chemical Company.

Danforth rehired Thomas as a legislative assistant in Washington, D.C., from 1979 to 1981, where he worked on energy issues for the Senate Commerce Committee.

Although they were ordained in different denominations, Thomas and Danforth had both studied to be ordained. Danforth was a big supporter of Clarence Thomas when he was running for the Supreme Court.

After Reagan's re-election in 1980, President Jimmy Carter nominated Thomas to serve as Assistant Secretary for Civil Rights at the Department of Education.

The Senate received Thomas' nomination on May 28, 1981, and he was confirmed on June 26, 1981, succeeding Cynthia Brown in the position. Harry Singleton succeeded Thomas. From 1982 to 1990, Thomas was the head of the Equal Employment Opportunity Commission (EEOC). According to journalist Evan Thomas, Thomas was "openly ambitious for higher office" during his time at the EEOC. Self-reliance was promoted by him as chairman of the EEOC, and class action lawsuits were halted in favor of pursuing acts of individual discrimination. According to the New York Times, he also claimed in 1984 that black leaders were "watching the destruction of our race" because they were "bitch, bitch, bitch" about Reagan instead of working together with the Reagan administration to alleviate issues such as teenage pregnancy.

THE FEDERAL JUDGE

Following the retirement of Robert Bork from the D.C. Circuit, President George H.W. Bush nominated Thomas on October 30, 1989.

Thomas's initial reluctance to serve as a judge was followed by this decision. "It was striking to me how easy it had become for sanctimonious [white] Democrats to accuse a black man of not caring about civil rights" when I met with white Democratic staffers in the United States Senate," Thomas said.

THE CONFIRMATION HEARING FOR THOMAS WENT OFF WITHOUT A HITCH.

On March 6, 1990, he was confirmed by the United States Senate and appointed by President George H.W. Bush. While serving on the Federal Court, he formed close friendships with other judges, including Ruth Bader Ginsburg.

NOMINATION AND CONFIRMATION TO THE SUPREME COURT OF THE UNITED STATES

In July 1990, when Associate Justice William Brennan announced his retirement from the Supreme Court, Thomas was Bush's top choice from among a short list of five candidates. That's why, after consulting with his team, Bush chose David Souter from the First Circuit. A year later, Bush nominated Thomas to succeed retiring Justice Thurgood Marshall, the Court's lone African American member. Bush described Thomas as the "best qualified at this time" when announcing his choice on July 1, 1991.

The American Bar Association (ABA) provides confidential ratings of judicial temperament, competence, and integrity on a three-level scale from "well qualified" to "qualified" or "unqualified" to U.S. presidents for potential federal court nominees.

As Adam Liptak of the New York Times pointed out, the American Bar Association has a history of taking liberal positions on contentious issues, and polls show that candidates nominated by Democratic presidents do better than those nominated by Republicans. Expecting the American Bar Association to rate Thomas lower than they believed was fair, the White House and Republican senators worked to have the ABA grant Thomas at least a mid-level qualified rating while also trying to discredit the ABA as partisan in its approach. Even though Thomas received the ABA's lowest level of support of any nominee to the Supreme Court, the organization still considered him qualified.

Some of Thomas's opponents' public statements foreshadowed his confirmation hearings. The nomination was approached as a political campaign by liberal interest groups and Republicans in the White House and Senate.

President Bush had been warned by Attorney General Richard Thornburgh earlier this year that any candidate who was not perceived to share Marshall's views would have a difficult time being confirmed as the next Attorney General.

Feminist and civil rights organizations opposed Thomas's appointment because of his criticism of affirmative action and his alleged disapproval of Roe v. Wade.

As of September 10, 1991, Thomas had begun his formal confirmation hearings.

After what happened to Robert Bork during his confirmation hearings four years earlier when he expounded on his judicial philosophy, he was wary of answering senators' questions during the process.

Prior to his confirmation hearings, Thomas frequently referred to natural law as a "philosophical background" to the U.S. Constitution in his writings and speeches.

Thomas's nomination was sent to the full Senate without recommendation on September 27, 1991, after a lengthy debate. Earlier in the day, a motion to recommend the nomination was defeated 7–7. There were Hill's sexual harassment allegations against Thomas made public after the committee reported the nomination.

BELIEFS AND ASSERTIONS ABOUT ANITA HILL

ANITA HILL HAS ACCUSED CLARENCE THOMAS OF SEXUAL HARASSMENT.

An FBI interview with Anita Hill was leaked to the press at the end of the committee's confirmation hearings and while the Senate was debating whether to give final approval to Thomas's nomination. It was postponed until October 8 as a result, and the confirmation hearings were reopened. There have been only three other occasions in Senate history when a nomination was recommitted to the Judiciary Committee, the last of which was in 1925, when Harlan F. Stone's nomination was recommitted.

Hill testified in front of the Judiciary Committee that Thomas had made sexual remarks to her ten years earlier, which she considered harassment because it was "behavior that is unbefitting an individual who will be a member of the Court."

While Hill was testifying, some senators interrogated her aggressively, bringing up some of the more graphic details of her past. To begin, Hill accused Thomas of making two sexist remarks to her: comparing his own penis to that of black pornstar Long Dong Silver and claiming that he found pubic hair on his Coca-Cola bottle.

Thomas was called back to testify before the panel. A statement by him: denying the accusations

Discussions about difficult topics should not be held in a private or closed environment at this time. A circus, indeed. It is a national disgrace. As a black American, I see it as a high-tech lynching for uppity blacks who dare to think for themselves, do for themselves, or have different ideas.

Thomas was unwavering in defense of his right to privacy throughout his deposition. Clearly, he didn't want to expose his private life to the public, allow the committee (or anyone else) to look into it, or describe any conversations with others about his private life. He had the right to do so, and the committee accepted that.

He had sexually harassed her, but Hill was the only one to publicly testify about it.

The former EEOC employee who was fired by Thomas decided not to testify.

Allegedly, he pressed her for a date and made comments about the female anatomy, but he didn't make her feel intimidated or sexually harassed, though she acknowledged that "some other women may have." Former Thomas assistant Sukari wrote a letter to a Senate panel Hardnett wrote: "If you were young, black, female and reasonably attractive, you knew full well that you were being inspected and auditioned as a female." — Sukari Hardnett

Hill and Thomas were just two of the many witnesses who appeared before the committee during its three-day hearings on October 11–13, 1991.

Nancy Altman, a former coworker of Thomas's at the Department of Education, testified that she was in the same room as Thomas for two years and never heard a sexist or offensive comment from him. Altman didn't believe Thomas' claim that no one among the dozens of women with whom he worked had witnessed his alleged misconduct. Sen. Alan K. Simpson asked why Hill met, dined, and spoke on the phone with Thomas on a number of occasions after they had no longer worked together, echoing some of the committee members' doubts. When Thomas wrote My Grandfather's Son: A Memoir in 2007, he addressed Hill's allegations and the caustic confirmation hearings.

Thomas "lied" to the Judiciary Committee about sexually harassing Anita Hill, Corey Robin, a journalist, wrote in a 2019 monograph, citing "evidence amassed by investigative journalists over... years," as well as new evidence, including corroborative testimony, that Thomas "subjected her to sexually harassing comments."

A genuine reaction to the accusations, Thomas believed, was his description of them as a "high-tech lynching" by the Judiciary Committee, which Robin agreed with.

THE SENATE VOTES

In a White House ceremony on October 23, 1991, Justice Byron White swore in Clarence Thomas as a member of the U.S. Supreme Court as his wife Virginia Thomas looked on.

Following Thomas' testimony, the Senate voted 52–48 on October 15, 1991, to confirm him as an associate justice of the Supreme Court.

With 46 Democrats and two Republicans voting to reject Thomas' nomination in the total number of votes cast, he received the support of 41 Republicans and 11 Democrats.

It was the second-longest period of time since 1975 that a nominee had to wait to be voted on in the Senate, after Bork's 108 days, and the narrowest margin of 24–23 since 1881, when Stanley Matthews was confirmed.

However, his tie-breaking vote did not help in the confirmation of the nominee, Dan Quayle, as president of the Senate.

On October 23, Thomas was sworn in as the 106th justice of the Supreme Court by taking the required oaths of office. Sadly, Chief Justice William Rehnquist's wife had passed away, so his oath-taking was postponed until after his swearing-in, which took place on November 1.

JUDICIAL THOUGHT AND PRACTICE

There is a difference between conservatism and originalism.

Originalist and textualist are two terms that are frequently used to describe Thomas.

He is frequently referred to as the Court's most conservative justice. However, Antonin Scalia was referred to as such by other justices while they were on the Court together. Commentators speculate about the extent to which Scalia found some of Thomas's views implausible, and Scalia was a staunch supporter of Thomas's judicial philosophy.

Justice Hugo Black, who "resisted the tendency to create social policy out of 'whole cloth,'" has been compared to Thomas's jurisprudence.

It's been argued elsewhere that Thomas is more interested in the Court's constitutional role as an interpreter of the law than a legislator.

Some critics claim that Thomas's jurisprudence is inconsistent in its application of originalism because they downplay the importance of originalism.

Thomas "will use originalism where it supports a politically conservative result," according to law professor Jim Ryan and former litigator Doug Kendall, but ignores originalism when "history provides no support" for a conservative ruling.

A "pluralistic approach to originalism" has been proposed by others, in which Thomas relies on the original intent, understanding, and public meaning of a text to make his decisions. When racial issues come up in court cases, critics say that Thomas' originalism often appears inconsistent or pluralistic. Thomas' interpretation of the Constitution is based on a narrative of originalism, according to Robin, which he describes as "at best episodic" in his rulings.

Alignment of votes

In his early years on the Court, Thomas tended to side with Scalia and Chief Justice William Rehnquist.

Scalia and Thomas' 87 percent voting alignment from 1994 to 2004 were the highest on the Court, closely followed by Ruth Bader Ginsburg and David Souter's 82 percent alignment (86 percent). Scalia and Thomas's agreement rate peaked in 1996 when they were both at 98%. Scalia and Thomas were no longer the only two justices who shared a strong ideological bond.

Linda Greenhouse's observation that Thomas voted with Scalia 91% of the time during October Term 2006 and with Justice John Paul Stevens the least, 36% of the time, confirms the conventional wisdom that Thomas's votes follow Scalia's.

Although Scalia frequently joined Thomas, Jan Crawford claims that this is also true in the other direction.

Statistics from SCOTUSblog show that Greenhouse's count is methodologically specific, counting cases where Scalia and Thomas voted for the same litigant, regardless of whether they reached that conclusion by using the same reasoning. There was only a 74% agreement rate, according to Goldstein's statistics, and the frequency of agreement between the two was far less impressive than many articles aimed at the general public would lead one to believe, While Souter and Ginsburg voted 81% of the time in unison, Thomas and Scalia were in unison on 74% of their votes during the same time period. According to the Scalia/Thomas metric, Ginsburg and Breyer agreed 91% of the time. 94% of the time, Roberts and Alito agreed. That Thomas followed Scalia's votes has been debunked by Robin, according to him.

Thomas's strong opinions, Crawford wrote in her book on the Supreme Court, pushed "moderates like Sandra Day O'Connor further to the left" but drew votes from Rehnquist and Scalia on numerous occasions.

Thomas's views, according to Mark Tushnet and Jeffrey Toobin, made it difficult for Rehnquist to persuade a majority of the Court to join him.

FREQUENCY OF DISSENTING VIEWPOINTS

As of the end of the 2019 term, Thomas had written 693 opinions, excluding opinions relating to orders or the "shadow docket ."There are 223 majority opinions, 226 concurrences, 214 dissents, and 30 "split" opinions in this total of 693 opinions. For the majority opinion, Thomas has written 40 times, and for the dissenting opinion, 30 times.

Thomas was the third-most frequent dissenter on the Supreme Court from 1994 to 2004, following Stevens and Scalia.

As many as four other justices dissented in 2007. There were also dissenting votes from three other justices in 2006. Another justice dissented just as often in 2005, if not more frequently.

TAKE A STAND

Stare decisis is the United States legal system is also discussed.

"Stare decisis provides continuity to our system, it provides predictability, and in our process of case-by-case decision-making, I think it is a very important and critical concept," said Thomas during his confirmation hearings.

"Thomas does not presume in making a final decision, regardless of the circumstances," Scalia says. He has a history of overruling precedent more frequently than any other justice on the Rehnquist Court, and this assessment is consistent with his record on the bench.

Moreover, Scalia claims that Thomas is more willing to overrule constitutional cases than he was in the past: "He would say that if the constitutional chain of command was incorrect, it should be rectified. Not in my wildest dreams!" Scalia's portrayal of Thomas, according to law professor Michael Gerhardt, may be inaccurate, given that Thomas has supported the preservation of a wide range of constitutional decisions. In the face of a conflict between Constitutional principles and a line of unreasoned cases wholly divorced from the text, history, and structure of our founding document, we should not hesitate to resolve the tension in favor of the Constitution's original meaning, says Thomas. No matter how old the decision is, Thomas believes that it should be overturned.

According to Amy Coney Barrett, then an assistant professor at Notre Dame Law School, Thomas is a proponent of the doctrine of statutory stare decisis. His dissenting opinion in Fogerty v. Fantasy was one of many examples cited by her.

A 5–4 decision by Thomas in Franchise Tax Board of California v. Hyatt (2019) overruled Nevada v. Hall (1979), which stated that states could be sued in other states' courts. According to him, it is not a "command" to follow one's conscience. Reliance on interests as a justification for adhering to precedent was explicitly disavowed by Thomas. During his dissent from the Franchise Tax Board of California, Justice Stephen Breyer suggested that Roe v. Wade might be one of the other decisions that might be overruled in the future. Prior precedent should be left alone unless it is widely regarded as incorrect or impractical.

A 7–2 decision in Flowers v. Mississippi (2019) found only Neil Gorsuch and Thomas disagreed with the ruling that overturned the death sentence of Mississippi resident Curtis Flowers, and Thomas suggested that the decision made in Batson v. Kentucky, which forbids the use of race in making peremptory challenges to jury selection, was wrong and should be overruled. Unlike Thomas, Gorsuch did not agree that Batson should be overruled.

For decades, Thomas has advocated a narrower interpretation of the Commerce Clause (also known as the Interstate Commerce Clause) to limit the federal government's power, even while broadening state sovereign immunity from lawsuits.

The Supreme Court ruled in the cases of United States v. Lopez and United States v. Morrison that Congress lacked the authority to regulate non-commercial activities under the Commerce Clause. A separate concurring opinion was written by Thomas in these cases in support of the Commerce Clause's original meaning. Later, in Gonzales v. Raich, the Supreme Court interpreted the Commerce Clause combined with the Necessary and Proper Clause as allowing the federal government to detain, prosecute, and imprison patients who use marijuana grown at home for medicinal purposes even if that is legal under state law. As in Raich, Thomas voiced his dissent, this time in support of the Commerce Clause's original intent.

The so-called "Negative Commerce Clause," which Thomas and Scalia called the "Dormant Commerce Clause," was rejected by the two justices. Even if Congress has not yet taken any action, this doctrine prevents the state from regulating commerce.

In Lopez, Thomas argued that the Commerce Clause does not apply to federal regulation of manufacturing and agriculture.

Some of his critics argue that his position on congressional authority would invalidate much of the federal government's current work, while he believes that federal legislators have overextended the Clause. Thomas argues that it is not the Court's role to keep the Constitution up-to-date and relevant. According to proponents like Professor Michael Dorf, they're not trying to do so; instead, they're simply addressing a set of economic facts that didn't exist when the Constitution was written.

FEDERALISM, EXECUTIVE POWER, AND FEDERAL STATUTES ALL FALL UNDER THE UMBRELLA OF FEDERALISM

According to Thomas, federal statutes and the Constitution give the executive branch broad powers. During Hamdi v. Rumsfeld, he was the only justice to agree with the Fourth Circuit that Congress had the authority to authorize the president's detention of U.S. citizens who are enemy combatants. A good-faith executive determination is all that is needed to establish a due process in the case of a U.S. citizen's detention, according to Thomas.

The military commissions at Guantanamo Bay required explicit congressional authorization and conflicted with both the Uniform Code of Military Justice (UCMJ) and "at least" Common Article Three of the Geneva Convention. Three justices disagreed with the majority, including Clarence Thomas in Hamdan v. Rumsfeld.

Scalia and Thomas both agreed that the Court was "patently erroneous" in its declaration of the jurisdiction in this case because Hamdan was an illegal combatant.

Thomas dissented from a denial of a stay application in the Ninth Circuit case East Bay Sanctuary Covenant v. Trump (2018), which placed an injunction on the Trump administration's asylum policy. To put an end to Trump's plan to grant asylum only to refugees who arrive at one of several designated ports, the Ninth Circuit Court issued an injunction, ruling that it violated the Immigration and Nationality Act of 1952. Denial of the ability to apply for asylum regardless of the entry point is "the hollowest of rights that an alien must be allowed to apply for asylum regardless if another rule makes her categorically ineligible for asylum based on precisely that fact," wrote the Ninth Circuit Judge Jay Bybee in the majority opinion of the case. Boris Berezovsky's appeal to the Supreme Court was rejected by Antonin Scalia, Samuel Alito, and Brett Kavanaugh.

FEDERALISM

The Rehnquist Court's constitutional agenda included a strong emphasis on federalism.

Federalism-based limits on the enumerated powers of Congress are an area where Thomas consistently supported outcomes that promoted state government authority. There has been no movement toward "the broader and more principled version of federalism propounded by Justice Thomas," according to law professor Ann Althouse.

Thomas dissents from the majority opinion in Foucha v. Louisiana, which mandated the removal of a sane prisoner from a mental institution.

 The Due Process Clause because it allows an insanity acquitted person to be committed to a mental institution, even though he or she does not suffer from any mental illness," the Court said in its decision. Thomas, in his dissent, framed the issue as one of federalism. Even though it may be a sound policy to remove those found not guilty of insanity in Court from mental institutions in some cases, the Due Process Clause does not require states to follow federal judges' preferences in this regard. Using federalism once more, Thomas' dissent in United States v. Comstock argued for the release of a formerly federal prisoner from civil commitment. A dissenting opinion in U.S. Term Limits Inc. v.

Thornton supported term limits for federal House and Senate candidates as a legitimate exercise of state legislative power.

LAWS PASSED BY THE FEDERAL GOVERNMENT

Although Thomas was willing to exercise judicial review of federal statutes in 2007, he was not as likely to overturn state statutes as other members of the Supreme Court at the time.

New York Times opinion piece, "between 1994 and 2005. Justice Thomas voted to overturn federal laws in 34 cases and Justice Scalia in 31, compared with just 15 for Justice Stephen Breyer."

Only Thomas voted to strike down Section 5 of the 1965 Voting Rights Act in the case of Northwest Austin Municipal Utility District No. 1 v. Holder. In Section Five, the Justice Department must approve any changes to election procedures in states that have a history of racial voter discrimination. As of 2006, Congress had voted to extend Section Five's lifespan by an additional 25 years, but Thomas argued that it was no longer necessary due to higher-than-average turnout among black voters in seven states covered by Section Five. That which prompted Congress to enact Section 5 and this court to uphold it is no longer in existence: violence, intimidation, and subterfuge, he claimed in his writing. In Shelby County v. Holder, he voted with the majority and agreed with the majority's reasoning that Section Five was unconstitutional.

Affirmative action, equality of protection, and racial profiling

Race-based affirmative action or preferential treatment is prohibited by Thomas' view of the Equal Protection Clause of the Fourteenth Amendment. For example, in Adarand Constructors v. Pea, he wrote: "Race-based policies that distribute benefits on the basis of race are morally and constitutionally equivalent to those that target a specific group of people in order to promote a current concept of equality. The only thing government can do is recognize, respect, and protect us as equals in the eyes of the law, not make us equal. No matter how well-intentioned the [affirmative action] programs may have been, they can't get around the constitutional prohibition against racial discrimination."

The Equal Protection Clause, Thomas wrote in Gratz v. Bollinger, "categorically prohibits a state from using racial discrimination in higher education admissions.

It was Thomas who agreed with Chief Justice Roberts that "the way to stop racism is to stop racism," in the case of Parents Involved in Community Schools v. Seattle School District No. 1. From the other side of the argument in the debate on the Supreme Court, Thomas wrote that "if our history has taught us anything, it has taught us to be wary of elites who hold racist views" and that dissenting views had "similarities" to those of the segregationists in Brown vs. Board of Education.

When it came to the case of Grutter v. Bollinger, Thomas quoted with approval from Justice Harlan's Plessy V. Ferguson dissent: "Our Constitution is color-blind and neither knows nor tolerates classes among citizens."

He wrote in Missouri v. Jenkins (1995) that the Missouri District Court erred in its interpretation of the Constitution and "has read our cases to support the theory that segregation harms black students' mental and educational development in an unspecified way. Not only does this approach use questionable social science research, but it also assumes that black people are inferior."

Race and the Constitution have been described by some legal scholars as "idiosyncratic," "pessimistic," or "fatalistic" Thomas.

According to professors Corey Robin and Stephen F. Smith, Thomas's philosophy is based on black nationalism, which views governmental efforts to combat racism as either futile or counterproductive. Racial discrimination is no longer a major issue in the United States, according to the opposite view, which holds that laws should be race-neutral.

FAMILY PLANNING AND ABORTION

Abortion is not explicitly mentioned in the US Constitution, according to Thomas.

The Supreme Court reaffirmed Roe v. Wade in Planned Parenthood v. Casey (1992). Rehnquist and Scalia joined Thomas and Justice Byron White in their dissent. According to Rehnquist, "we believe Roe was wrongly decided, and that it can and should be overruled."

A state ban on partial-birth abortion was struck down by the Supreme Court in Stenberg v. Carhart (2000) because it did not meet the "undue burden" standard established in Casey. Disagreeing with the majority, Thomas wrote, "Although a State may permit abortion, nothing in the Constitution dictates that a State must do so." "To conceal its anti-abortion hostility, the majority's insistence on an exception for health reasons is only "a fig leaf barely covering its antipathy to any abortion regulation by the States—a hostility that Casey purported to reject."

Accompanied by colleagues, Thomas said that the Court had no basis in the Constitution for its abortion jurisprudence but that the Court was correct in applying it in rejecting the challenge. He asserted that the parties hadn't raised or briefed this issue and that it isn't relevant to the question at hand. Additionally, the lower courts haven't addressed it either. "The question of whether the Act falls within the Commerce Clause's purview is not before the Court. That issue was not brought up or briefed by the parties."

He dissented in December of last year when the Supreme Court rejected two states' appeals against Planned Parenthood's denial of Medicaid funding.

To Alito and Gorsuch, the Court was "abdicating its judicial duty," as Thomas put it in his dissenting dissent.

Thomas and three other conservative justices on the Supreme Court rejected a temporary restraining order against a Louisiana law restricting abortion in February 2019.

In a 5–4 decision, the Supreme Court stayed a law that would have required doctors who perform abortions to have hospital admitting privileges.

As part of a per Curiam decision upholding an Indiana abortion restriction regarding the disposal of the remains and upholding the lower court rulings striking down the provision banning race, gender, and disability, Thomas argued that the practice of eugenics, which was practiced in the United States and by the

Nazis in the early 20th century, was similar to abortion and birth control in the early 20th century. The horrors of "abortion and infanticide," in Margaret Sanger's words (as quoted by Thomas), led Sanger to advocate contraception as a superior method of personal reproductive control. When Thomas cited Adam Cohen's book Imbeciles: The Supreme Court, American Eugenics, and the Sterilization of Carrie Buck in his opinion, the historian/journalist responded with a scathing critique, claiming that Thomas had misunderstood Cohen and the history of the eugenics movement in general. Just Ruth Bader Ginsberg and Sonia Sotomayor publicly voted in Box. A majority of Ginsburg's and Sotomayor's opinions were in agreement with the lower Court's decisions, but they were divided on whether or not to uphold the ban on the disposal of fetal remains due to race, sex, and disability.

Courts should revisit precedents like Griswold (1965), Lawrence v. Texas (2003), and Obergefell v. Hodges (2012); Thomas wrote in his concurring opinion for the Dobbs case in 2022. (2015). Sodomy, homosexuality, and same-sex marriage would all be made illegal if these rulings were overturned.

THE RIGHTS OF LESBIAN, GAY, BISEXUAL,

According to Thomas, the federal government unlawfully entrapped a gay man when it enticed him into purchasing a magazine containing nude pictures of underage boys in Jacobson v. United States (1992).

Scalia's dissenting opinion argued that Amendment Two to the Colorado State Constitution did not violate the Equal Protection Clause in Romer v. Evans (1996). In order to protect people from discrimination based on "homosexual, lesbian, or bisexual orientation, conduct, practices or relationships," the Colorado amendment forbade any judicial or legislative action.

In Lawrence v. Texas (2003), Thomas wrote a one-page dissent in which he used the phrase "uncommonly silly" first used by Justice Stewart to describe the Texas statute prohibiting sodomy. It was then stated that he would vote to repeal the law if he were in the Texas legislature because it was a waste of "law enforcement resources" to monitor private sexual activity. Because he believed that there was no constitutional right to privacy, Thomas abstained from voting to overturn the law. He viewed it as a matter for individual states to decide.

He was joined by Alito and Kavanaugh in dissenting from the decision that the Civil Rights Act of 1964 protects employees from discrimination based on sexual orientation or gender identity in the case of Bostock v. Clayton County, Georgia (2020). Kavanaugh wrote his own dissent (Thomas and Alito wrote a joint dissent). There were two Republicans, Roberts, and Gorsuch, and four Democrats, Ginsburg, Breyer, Sotomayor, and Elena Kagan, in the majority of the 6–3 decision.

Even though Thomas voted to reject Kim Davis' appeal from the county clerk who refused to issue marriage licenses to same-sex couples, the Supreme Court justice wrote an opinion reiterating his disdain for Obergefell and saying that he believes it was wrongly decided by the High Court.

One of three justices, Gorsuch and Alito, voted to hear an appeal from a same-sex couple in Washington State who had refused service because of their religious beliefs against same-sex marriage in July 2021. In November 2021, the Supreme Court rejected an appeal from Mercy San Juan Medical Center, a Catholic-affiliated hospital, 6-3. Thomas dissented from the majority of justices. As a result of Alito and Gorsuch's dissents, the appeal was rejected, leaving in place a lower court decision in favor of the patient.

FAMILY AND FRIENDS

The name of Jamal Adeen. Thomas's lone child was born in 1973 in New Haven, Connecticut. In 1981, Thomas and his first wife divorced, and it was in 1984 that he remarried. His first wife was a lobbyist and Dick Armey's chief of staff, Virginia Lamp. Thomas's great-nephew Mark Martin Jr., who was six years old at the time, had been living in public housing in Savannah with his mother. A motorcoach has transported Thomas and his wife since 1999 as they alternate between court appearances across the United States.

Throughout her political career, Virginia "Ginni" Thomas has served as a consultant to the Heritage Foundation and as the president of Liberty Central.

With her experience and connections, she left Liberty Central in 2011 to open her conservative lobbying firm, meeting with newly elected Republican representatives and claiming to be a "Tea Party ambassador." House Democrats wrote to Justice Thomas' office in 2011 saying that because of his wife's work on the Affordable Care Act, there appeared to be a conflict of interest, and he should recuse himself from those cases.

Common Cause reported in January 2011 that between 2003 and 2007, Thomas failed to disclose $686,589 in income his wife earned from the Heritage Foundation, instead of reporting "none" where "spousal noninvestment income" would be reported on his Supreme Court financial disclosure forms.

 When asked about it the following week, Thomas claimed that his wife's earnings had been "inadvertently omitted due to a misunderstanding of the filing instructions." He made changes to old reports dating back to 1989.

According to the Washington Post, Ginni Thomas apologized to former clerks of Thomas on the email listserv "Thomas Clerk World" in February 2021 for her role in contributing to the "pro-Trump postings and former Thomas clerk John Eastman, who spoke at the rally and represented Trump in some of his failed lawsuits filed to overturn the election results," which had caused a rift.

Select Committee on the January 6 Attack received text messages between Ginni Thomas and Trump's chief of staff, Mark Meadows, from 2020 to March 2022. In a series of text messages, Ginni Thomas urged Meadows to overturn the election results and recited conspiracy theories about ballot fraud. Ginni Thomas' involvement in efforts to overturn the results of the 2020 presidential election and the January 6 attack on the U.S. Capitol raises questions about Thomas's impartiality, according to 24 Democratic Congress and the Senate.

According to a Quinnipiac poll conducted in April 2022, half of all Americans believe Ginni Thomas's texts about overturning the results of the 2020 presidential election require him to step down from all cases involving presidential elections.

RELIGION

In the mid-1990s, Clarence Thomas made amends with the Catholic Church.

When confronted with racism during the civil rights movement in the 1960s, he wrote in his autobiography that the church was "not so adamant about ending racism then as it is about ending abortion now" in dealing with the issue. There have been 14 practicing Catholic justices on the Supreme Court, and Thomas is one of six serving today (along with Alito, Kavanaugh, Roberts, Sotomayor, and Barrett).

ACCUSATIONS OF HARASSMENT

An attorney who worked for the Truman Foundation in 1999, Moira Smith, claimed in 2016 that Thomas groped her during an informal dinner party. Thomas described the claim as "ridiculous."

__________ THE END ________

www.ingramcontent.com/pod-product-compliance
Lightning Source LLC
Chambersburg PA
CBHW060916130726
48001CB00006B/2265